The Missing Masks

Written by
Liz Miles

Illustrated by
Howard McWilliam

In this story:

Jay

Sniffer

Mr Slime   The teacher

The school hall got very wet.

"It will cost a lot to fix the hall," said the teacher. "We will have to shut the school."

"Let's put on a play," said Jay.
"People will pay to see it.
Then we can fix the hall!"

"I will take the duck masks and stop the play," said Mr Slime.

8

"Then the school will shut and
I can put a hotel here! People
will pay a lot to stay in it."

It was the day of the play.
The children went to get their masks.

"Oh no! Where are the masks?" said Jay.
Just then, there was a sneeze.

Aaachoo!

Sniffer ran to get Jay.
"Oh no! Mr Slime has got the masks!"
said Jay. "Quick, Sniffer! Let's get him!"

Aaachoo!

Jay got on his bike. Sniffer got on too. They followed Mr Slime into the park.

Mr Slime let go of the masks.
He fell into the pond.

Splash!

"This is a better place for the play!" said Jay. "People will pay a lot to see it here. Thank you, Mr Slime!"